REPTILES FOR KIDS

REPTILES FOR KIDS

A JUNIOR SCIENTIST'S GUIDE
to Lizards, Amphibians, and Cold-Blooded Creatures

JUNIOR SCIENTISTS

MICHAEL G. STARKEY

ROCKRIDGE PRESS

To my parents: For believing in my abilities and allowing me the opportunity to follow my passion for reptiles . . . including the boa constrictor that escaped into the air-conditioning vents of the family car.

For general information on our other products and services or to obtain technical support, please contact our Customer Care Department within the United States at (866) 744-2665, or outside the United States at (510) 253-0500.

Rockridge Press publishes its books in a variety of electronic and print formats. Some content that appears in print may not be available in electronic books, and vice versa.

Interior and Cover Designer: Gabe Nansen
Art Producer: Tom Hood
Editor: Sabrina Young
Production Editor: Mia Moran

Illustrations: Conor Buckley, © 2020, pp. 2, 9, 14, 15, 29, 44, 56, 66; Kate Francis, © 2020 p 16; Andrey Atuchin, p 63; Photography David Kenny/Science Source, pp. ii, iii, 35, 36; Gerdzhikov/iStock, p vi; Biosphoto/Science Source, pp. viii, 1, 11, 12, 13, 54, 55, 74, 75; Wilkinson M, Sherratt E, Starace F, Gower DJ, p 4; Sebastian Janicki/Shutterstock, p 5; Ardea/Science Source, p 6; Joe Blossom/Alamy, pp. 7, 23; Danita Delimont/Alamy, p 8; Jason Ondreicka/Alamy, p 8; Scubazoo/Alamy, pp. 10, 53; GlobalP/iStock, p 15; bdspn/iStock, p 17; GlobalP/iStock, pp. 18, 68; Vasiliy Vishnevskiy/Alamy, p 20; Prakaymas Vitchitchalao, p 21; Matthijs Kuijpers/Alamy, pp. 22, 25, 33; Scott Camazine/Alamy, p 24; Design Pics/Science Source, pp. 26, 27; Stephen Dalton/Science Source, p 28; Freder/iStock, p 28; TomekD76/iStock p 29; Francesco Tomasinelli/Science Source, p 29; russaquarius/iStock, p 30; Robert Eastman/alamy, p 32; Prisma by Dukas Presseagentur GmbH/Alamy, p 34; Michael McCoy/Science Source, p 37; Life on white/Alamy, p 38; hsvrs/iStock, p 39; Mike Lane/Alamy, p 40; Wolfgang Kaehler/Alamy, p 41; UroshPetrovic/iStock, pp. 42, 43; Paul Whitten/Science Source, p 44; 4FR/iStock, p 45; Michael O'Neill/Science Source, p 46; Juan Aunion/Alamy, p 48; Victor Abbot/Alamy, p 49; blickwinkel/Alamy, p 50; fishHook Photography/Alamy, p 51; Brian Kushner/Alamy, p 52; Stephen Barnes/Animals/Alamy, p 57; Danita Delimont/Alamy, p 57; Pascal Goetgheluck/Science Source, p 58; reptiles4all/iStock, p 59; Natalia Kuzmina/Alamy, p 60; Anthony Vasseur/iStock, p 61; Byronsdad/iStock, p 62; alptraum/iStock, pp. 64, 65; Ted M. Kinsman/Science Source, p 66; FatCamera/iStock, p 67; Dave M Hunt Photography/iStock, p 69; randimal/iStock, p 70; Tom McHugh/Science Source, p 71.

Author photo courtesy of © Maaike Starkey

ISBN: Print 978-1-64739-649-7 | eBook 978-1-64739-650-3

RO

Printed in China

CONTENTS

Fire Salamander
(Salamandra salamandra)

WELCOME, JUNIOR SCIENTIST!

I have been obsessed with reptiles and amphibians my whole life. What's not to love? Reptiles are scaly and cold-blooded, and they have spikes and plates. These animals are amazing. As a child growing up in the city, I loved visiting the local zoo and kept pet reptiles in my bedroom. As I grew older, I was excited to learn that there are jobs for people who want to spend their days working with reptiles and amphibians. I am now a wildlife biologist. From studying frogs in Central America to working with wildlife conservation groups that protect snakes around the world, I have been lucky to travel the globe and meet the most amazing reptiles and amphibians. Guess what? You can too! If you love reptiles, reading this book is a great way to start your future career as a scientist.

Jackson's Chameleon
(Trioceros jacksonii)

Chapter One

WHAT IS A REPTILE?

Reptiles are ancient animals that have lived on Earth for a long, long time. The earliest reptile fossil we know of is estimated to be around 315 million years old. Since that time, reptiles have dominated the planet and today can be found on every continent except Antarctica. Reptiles thrive in many different **ecosystems**, from the hottest deserts to the middle of the ocean. These scaly animals come in a variety of shapes and sizes. Some reptiles are giants, and some are so small they can fit on the end of your fingernail. Reptiles can have beautiful colors and they can be masters of camouflage. Some are even venomous. Reptiles are a fascinating group of animals. Let's learn about them together.

The Reptile Family

As there are so many different types of reptiles, scientists work hard to name them all. To do this, they separate them into groups based on characteristics they share. This process of classifying reptiles and other groups of organisms is called **taxonomy**.

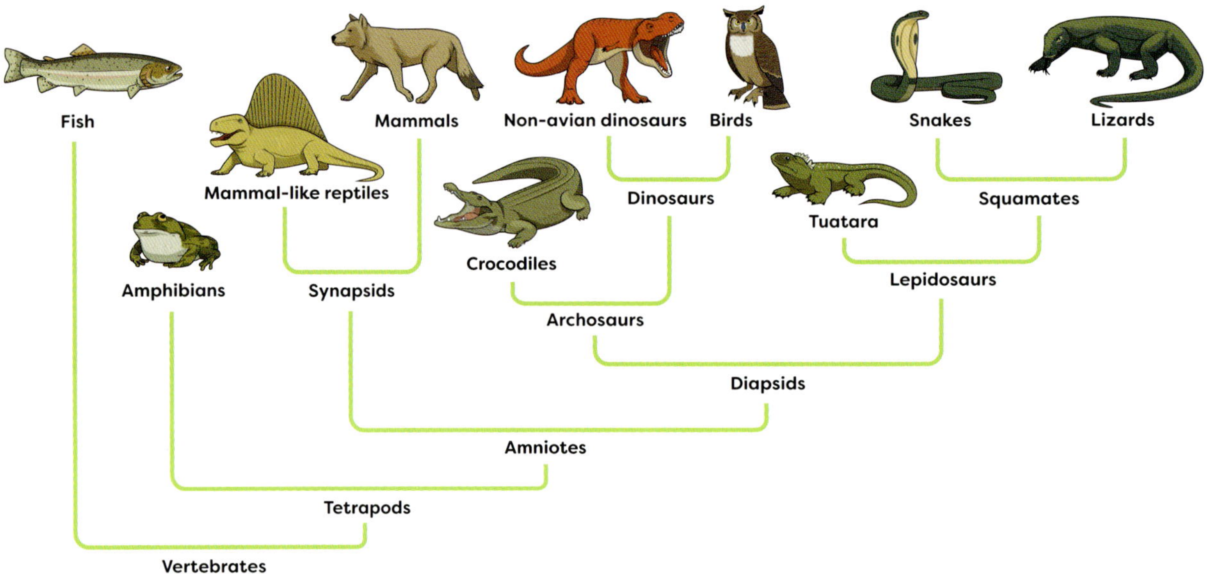

People from all around the world use different names for certain reptiles. All these common names can be very confusing. So, scientists give reptiles and other organisms a two-word scientific name, also called a Latin name. That way, we all know what reptile species we are talking about.

In this book, we will name reptiles with one of their common names, followed by their scientific name, which will always be in *italics*.

Here is an example of the taxonomy of a snake called the neotropical sunbeam (*Loxocemus bicolor*):

- This snake is an animal, so it is in the **kingdom** Animalia.
- This snake has a backbone, so it is in the **phylum** Chordata.
- This snake is a reptile, so it is in the **class** Reptilia.
- All snakes belong to the **order** Squamata, which actually contains snakes and lizards. So, they are also put into a **suborder** called Serpentes.
- This snake is the only member of the family Loxocemidae and so its **genus** is *Loxocemus*.
- The snake's pattern is dark on top and light on the bottom, so its **species** is *bicolor*.

How Reptiles and Amphibians Are Different

Amphibians and reptiles might look similar, but they are actually very different. While both groups are **vertebrates**, they are separated by millions of years of **evolution**.

Amphibians mostly live in wet environments. Their skin acts like a sponge to soak up moisture so that their bodies don't dry out. Most amphibians lay soft, jelly-like eggs and some species have a **larval** stage when young, like a tadpole, before they become adults through **metamorphosis**. Reptiles can thrive in different types of ecosystems because of their tough bodies. Their skin is covered with scales, which protect them from the elements and from drying out. After they're born, reptiles are ready to take on the world. These adaptations allow reptiles to live in many places where amphibians cannot.

CAECILIANS

What the heck is a caecilian? A caecilian is an amazing limbless amphibian. There are just over 200 different species around the world, and they are found throughout the tropical rain forests of Central and South America, Africa, and Asia.

Caecilians have poor vision because they live underground in burrows or in water, which means that they can usually only detect light and dark. Their pointed snout helps them burrow through dirt and mud. Some species are as small as earthworms, while others can grow to be five feet long.

What do they eat? When in **captivity**, they will eat worms, but other than that, we don't know. Scientists are still learning about these mysterious amphibians.

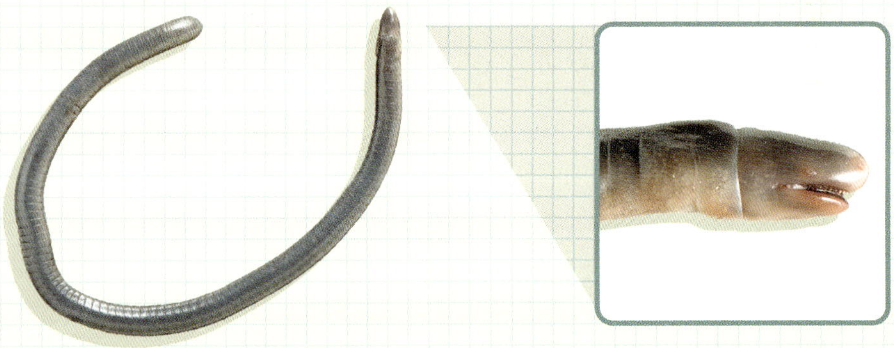

From Tip to Tail

Reptiles include turtles, tortoises, crocodilians (crocodiles, alligators, and caimans), snakes, **amphisbaenians**, lizards, and the tuatara. The tuatara is an ancient reptile that looks similar to a lizard, but it is part of a distinct lineage, the order Rhynchocephalia, and only lives in New Zealand. There are more than 10,000 species of reptiles around the world and scientists are still discovering new species!

Much of what makes a reptile a reptile is its anatomy. Reptiles are cold-blooded, which means they rely on their environment to help them regulate their body temperature. Reptiles are covered in unique skin and scales that protect them from harm.

SKIN AND SCALES

Reptiles grow continuously throughout their lives. This means that they need to shed their skin as they age, a process called **ecdysis**. Reptiles shed in different ways. Snakes will shed their skin by rubbing their noses on rocks or bark, which causes the skin to split and roll off in one piece. Lizards shed their skin in many pieces, bits at a time. Even turtles and tortoises shed the skins on their shells bit by bit as their new shell grows larger underneath.

Scales are made of **keratin**, just like our fingernails. Scales keep a reptile's skin from drying out and also serve as armor that helps protect them from predators or their environment. On snakes and lizards, the skin is covered in scales that overlap each other, like shingles on a roof. Turtles and crocodilians have thicker scales, called **scutes**, that do not overlap. Some scales are very special, like the long spines on the back of the green iguana.

MAKING SENSE

Reptiles communicate with each other in a variety of ways and for many different purposes. Most reptiles do not make noise, but rather use physical behaviors to "talk." Lizards have been observed doing push-ups, head bobbing, and even waving their arms at other lizards or potential predators. Chameleons use their incredible ability to change color to communicate with other chameleons. When the red-eared slider turtle male seeks the attention of a female, he will shake his long fingernails in front of her face. Geckos are among the few reptiles that communicate by making noise. They warn other geckos to stay out of their territories with a series of chirps, clicks, and squeaks.

Komodo Dragon *(Varanus komodoensis)*

KEEPING COOL

Reptiles are cold-blooded (**ectothermic**) and rely on the temperature in their environment to keep their bodies warm or cool. How do they do this? The sun! **Diurnal** reptiles are active during the day and will bask in the sun's rays to warm their bodies. Reptiles that are active at night (**nocturnal**) will heat up on rocks and other structures that were warmed by the sun.

As the seasons change, reptiles must deal with the cold. Maybe you have heard of hibernating? Reptiles do this, too, but scientists have a special word for hibernation of reptiles: **brumation**. During brumation, reptiles hide in deep burrows, hollowed-out trees, or caves—anywhere the temperature remains constant and cool. A reptile may use the same spot repeatedly year after year, decade after decade.

All reptiles need to rest and recharge. Some of their sleep patterns are similar to birds, humans, and other mammals. Some research suggests that lizards may even dream!

The Life of a Reptile

Reptiles have many different reproductive habits. When a male reptile is ready, he will try to mate with a female in many interesting ways. Male snakes, for example, search for the female by following her scent. If two male monitor lizards encounter a female, they might fight for the chance to mate with her.

Whereas some reptiles give birth to live young, most species lay soft-shelled eggs, which must be kept warm, or **incubated**, until they hatch. Some reptiles, like iguanas, leave their eggs shortly after they are laid, while other reptile species, like alligators, stay with the eggs until they hatch. Many lizards and snakes, including boa constrictors, give birth to live young (similar to how humans are born). Reptiles start life as miniature versions of their parents and are fully prepared to live in the wild.

MOVING ALONG

Reptiles use different forms of **locomotion** to move through their environments. Lizards walk on four legs, but some species, like the green basilisk (*Basiliscus plumifrons*), can run upright on their hind legs when they need to move fast. Snakes and legless lizards, like the eastern glass lizard (*Ophisaurus ventralis*), move using their incredibly strong muscles and belly scales. Many reptiles, like sea turtles, are excellent swimmers, perfectly adapted to life in the ocean.

When detected by a potential predator, many reptiles quickly flee. Some reptile species, like the Jackson's chameleon (*Trioceros jacksonii*), have excellent camouflage and can blend into their surroundings to hide from predators. To intimidate predators, reptiles like monitor lizards inflate their bodies with air to look bigger than they really are. They also defend themselves with a painful bite. Turtles and tortoises have hard shells to protect them from harm.

Green Basilisk *(Basiliscus plumifrons)*

Eastern Glass Lizard *(Ophisaurus ventralis)*

REPTILE TRACKS

It takes a careful eye to identify reptile tracks. The trick is to know what to look for. In lizard tracks, in between the footprints is a line, caused by the tail dragging behind. Alligators have a distinctive footprint, with five toes on the front feet and four toes on the back feet. Their tracks are usually accompanied by a tail drag, just like lizards. Turtle and tortoise footprints are usually rounded, but you might see the print of small toes. Look for turtle tracks near water. Snakes have probably the easiest track to identify because their bodies make a single line. However, some snakes, like the sidewinder (*Crotalus cerastes*), have unique tracks that zigzag across the desert sand.

THE REPTILE DIET

Reptiles are exceptional predators. A reptile's prey depends on its environment, but reptiles feast on a variety of prey, from insects and fish to amphibians, other reptiles, birds, and mammals. Some reptiles are specialized to eat a specific type of prey. One of the largest reptiles on the planet, the leatherback sea turtle (*Dermochelys coriacea*), feeds mostly on jellyfish. Depending on the size of the food item, it may take a few days or even weeks for the reptile to digest. Large pythons may only eat one large prey item per year.

Not all reptiles are carnivores. Some reptile species are dependent on leaves, cacti, grasses, and fruits for their meals. Large land tortoises, which can be found all around the world, are strictly vegetarians. Marine iguanas (*Amblyrhynchus cristatus*) live on the Galápagos Islands off the coast of Ecuador and dive underwater to feed on seaweed that grows on rocks.

Leatherback Sea Turtle
(Dermochelys coriacea)

Reptiles at Home and in the Wild

Reptiles live all over the world. If you spend time in nature, you might see reptiles in the wild. However, like any wild animal, reptiles deserve plenty of space and respect. Some reptiles, like alligators and venomous snakes, are potentially dangerous. After you spot a reptile, stop and observe it from a safe distance. Doing so will give you the opportunity to observe interesting behaviors that you might not have seen if you disturbed the animal.

It is an amazing experience to see a reptile in the wild, but it might not always be possible. Reptiles are secretive and can be difficult to find. Or, you might live in a city that is far from nature. If that is the case, consider checking out your local zoo or nature center. These organizations usually have some reptile ambassadors that you can learn about and see up close.

Central Bearded Dragons
(Pogona vitticeps)

Thai Bamboo Rat Snake
(Oreocryptophis porphyraceus)

Chapter Two

SNAKES

Today, we know of 3,800 species of snakes around the world. They come in all shapes and sizes. Even though they do not have limbs, these reptiles can slither, climb, swim, burrow, and glide! The ancestors of today's snakes once had legs, but through millions of years of evolution, snakes have perfected the art of being limbless. You might think this is a disadvantage, but a snake's unique anatomy helps it to survive in the wild.

Anatomy

A snake's skeleton is very different from that of other reptiles. Snakes' skeletons are made up of a skull, a spinal column, and hundreds of ribs. Because snakes do not have arms or legs, they do not have shoulder or hip bones.

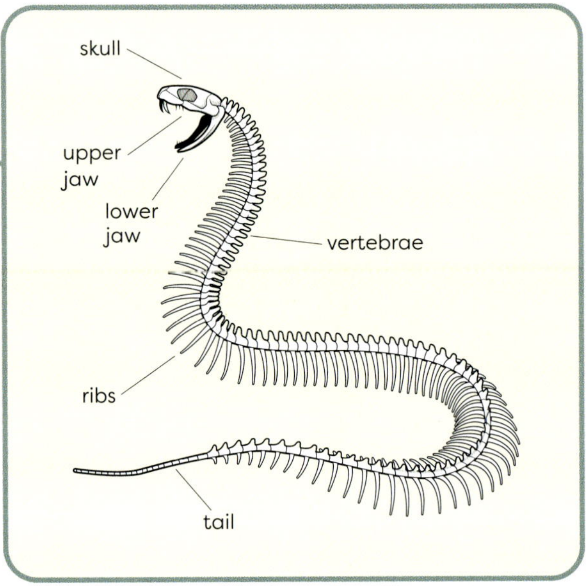

Snakes' organs are long and narrow, just like their bodies. Snakes have lungs, but in most species one lung is tiny and not functional.

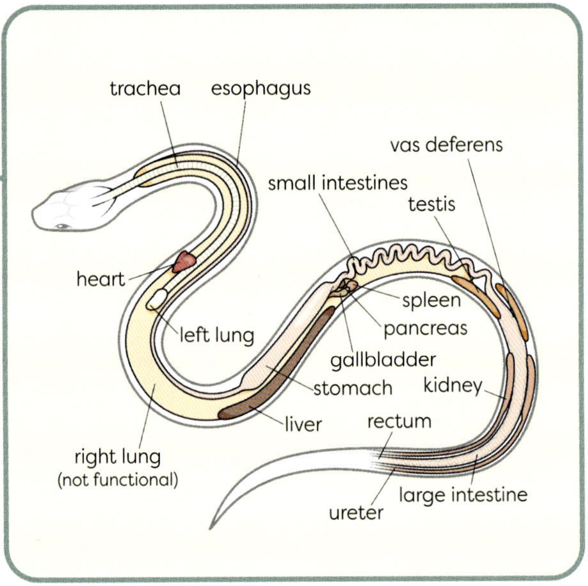

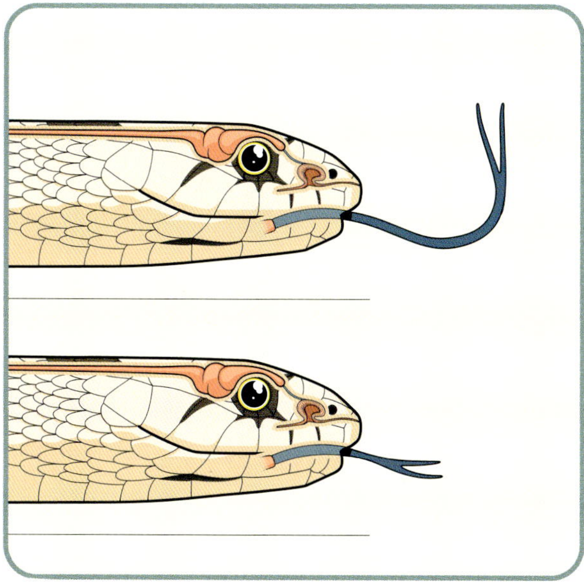

The most interesting part of a snake's anatomy is its forked tongue, which is connected to the vomeronasal, also called the **Jacobson's organ**. This sensory organ allows snakes to taste the air with their tongue. As the snake flicks its tongue, it picks up scent particles. This helps the snake to follow (or avoid) scents in its environment.

Emerald Tree Boa
(Corallus caninus)

Skin and Scales

Like other reptiles, snakes are covered in scales. Scales are made of keratin, just like your fingernails. The scales on top of the snake, or **dorsal** scales, are different from the scales on the bottom of the snake, the **ventral** scales. Dorsal scales act like armor and protect the snake from getting hurt. The ventral scales allow the snake to move. Snakes' scales are attached to each other by **interstitial** skin, which can be very hard to see. However, this skin is very stretchy and can be seen in between the scales after the snake has eaten a meal.

Every species of snake has a different color or pattern on their skin and scales; the pattern is helpful for camouflage or to warn potential predators that they may be venomous.

What They Eat

Snakes are predators and carnivores; they eat other animals to survive. Some nonvenomous snake species, like boas and pythons, use their strong bodies to overpower their prey. Other snakes, like rattlesnakes and cobras, are highly venomous; a bite from either can be deadly. After a snake has eaten a meal, it must digest its food. Depending on the size of this food item, it may take a few days or even weeks to digest!

Reptiles in the Wild

Like many wildlife species, some snakes are threatened, endangered, or on the brink of extinction. However, sometimes a species from another part of the world is introduced into a new habitat and does well . . . sometimes too well. When this happens, the introduced species can become an **invasive species**.

The Burmese python (*Python bivittatus*) is **native** to Asia but was introduced into the United States as a popular pet. These large pythons can grow to be more than 15 feet long, though—that's a pretty big to be a pet! In southern Florida, some pet owners released their "pets" into the wild, and the python population exploded, which is a problem for the native wildlife.

Burmese Python *(Python bivittatus)*

Although these snakes are thriving in the United States, in their native home of Asia, their population is in decline. The Burmese python is a threatened species because it is overharvested for its beautiful skin and it is losing its rain forest habitat. Fortunately, dedicated conservation groups in Southeast Asia are working to save these snakes and reduce the threats that are endangering their habitats.

REPTILES AT HOME

The gentle **ball python** and the farm-friendly **corn snake** are snakes that can be useful for budding herpetologists (someone who studies reptiles and amphibians) to study. Where can you go to learn more about these snakes—maybe even touch one? Find a local herpetological society where you can meet other snake fans, people who find snakes in the wild, or those who keep them at home. Search online to see if there's a herpetological society in your area. Zoos and nature centers may also have cool snakes that you can look at or touch.

Caring for a snake is a lot of responsibility. If you think you want a pet snake, do your research. Some snakes can grow very big very fast! Certain snakes don't do well in captivity. The ball python and the corn snake are popular pets because they are small, nonvenomous, and are bred in captivity. These snakes will grow to between four and five feet long, so they don't get too big. However, they do need to eat rodents and live in an enclosure that is big enough for them to stretch.

Fully understanding the needs of these snake species helps them live happy, healthy lives for many years.

Ball Python

Python regius

SAY IT! *PY-thon REE-juss*

The nonvenomous ball python is named for its interesting defense mechanism. When the snake is threatened, it rolls into a ball to protect its head. Like other pythons, ball pythons have openings in their jaw that can "see" heat! These heat pits allow the snake to detect warm-bodied prey and even predators.

Ball pythons are often hunted and sold as pets, which means that there are fewer living in the wild. Luckily, young ball pythons that are born in captivity make it possible to keep these snakes as pets without needing to hunt them in the wild. The ball python is pretty small (adults rarely reach six feet) and gentle, which makes it one of the most popular pet pythons.

REPTILE STATS

FAMILY NAME: Pythonidae (PY-thon-uh-dee)

HABITAT: Grasslands in West and Central Africa

SIZE: Up to 6 feet

COLOR: Bodies are black to dark brown with light brown blotches

DIET: Mammals

Corn Snake

Pantherophis guttatus

SAY IT! *PAN-ther-OH-fis GOO-tah-tuhs*

The corn snake is a medium-size, non-venomous snake from North America. It is a member of a group of snakes called "rat snakes." Can you guess what they love to eat? Rodents! They overpower their prey with their bodies using a method called constriction.

This snake is a farmer's best friend because it hunts the rats and mice that might destroy crops. In fact, corn snakes get their name because they are often found on farms near corn and grain silos, where mice and rats like to eat. These calm snakes are also very popular pets.

REPTILE STATS

FAMILY NAME: Colubridae (kuh-LOO-bruh-dee)

HABITAT: Woodlands, grasslands, and agricultural areas in the southeastern United States

SIZE: Up to 6 feet

COLOR: Orange with black lines and red markings on the back and a white-and-black checkered belly

DIET: Rodents, birds, reptiles, and amphibians

Black Mamba

Dendroaspis polylepis

SAY IT! *den-DROE-ahs-piz pohl-ee-LEEP-iss*

The black mamba is the second-longest venomous snake in the world, slightly shorter than the king cobra. Black mambas are fast—they can slither up to 12 miles per hour. Like other members of the Elapidae family, the black mamba has a highly venomous bite, with neurotoxic venom that is harmful to the brain and nervous system.

To warn potential predators, the black mamba will flatten its neck, hiss loudly, and open its mouth, which is black inside! The black mamba has a reputation for being highly aggressive but will only attack when threatened.

REPTILE STATS

FAMILY NAME: Elapidae (uh-LOP-uh-dee)

HABITAT: Savannah and woodland in sub-Saharan Africa

SIZE: Up to 14 feet

COLOR: Ranges in coloration, including olive, yellowish-brown, and gray

DIET: Mammals, birds, and reptiles

Boa Constrictor

Boa constrictor

SAY IT! *BOH-uh kun-STRIK-ter*

The common boa (also called a boa constrictor) is a large, nonvenomous constrictor in the family Boidae. This species includes many **subspecies** that live across the Americas. Some subspecies are small and only live on islands in the Caribbean Ocean, while other larger subspecies thrive in the rain forests of South America and can be up to 13 feet long.

The common boa is also called the red-tailed boa because the snake sometimes has a deep red, saddle-like pattern near its tail.

REPTILE STATS

FAMILY NAME: Boidae (BOH-uh-dee)

HABITAT: Forests, streams, or rivers in southern North America, Central America, and South America.

SIZE: 3 to 14 feet

COLOR: Brown, gray, or light tan with dark or reddish saddle-like patterns across the body

DIET: Birds, reptiles, and mammals

Cottonmouth

Agkistrodon piscivorus

SAY IT! *ag-KIS-truh-DON PIH-sih-VER-uhs*

The cottonmouth is a medium-size pit viper that is native to the southeastern United States. It is famous for its remarkable threat display. When cornered by a predator, the cottonmouth will coil itself into a strike position, inflate its body, and open its mouth! This shows off not only its fangs, but also the inside of its mouth, which is ivory white!

There are stories about cottonmouths being very aggressive, but these stories are untrue. Snakes are not aggressive; however, they will defend themselves when necessary.

REPTILE STATS

FAMILY NAME: Viperidae (VY-per-uh-dee)

HABITAT: Wetlands in the southeastern United States

SIZE: 3 to 5 feet

COLOR: Light and dark brown crossbands; some bodies are black or dark brown

DIET: Fish and amphibians

King Cobra

Ophiophagus hannah

SAY IT! *ah-FEE-ah-fuh-guhs HAN-nuh*

At 18 feet long, the king cobra is the longest venomous snake species in the world. King cobras live in large forests throughout South and Southeast Asia. They are the only species to make a nest in fallen leaves, which the snake uses to keep its eggs warm and safe. A mother king cobra will actively protect her nest from predators and will chase away any animal that gets too close.

With its impressive size and fascinating features, the king cobra is one of the most famous snake species. However, these snakes are shy and prefer to avoid humans. Due to loss of their forest habitat and increased contact with humans, king cobras are under threat of extinction.

REPTILE STATS

FAMILY NAME: Elapidae (uh-LOP-uh-dee)	**COLOR:** Gray to olive-green with black and white bands
HABITAT: Rain forests in South and Southeast Asia	**DIET:** Snakes and (occasionally) monitor lizards
SIZE: Up to 18 feet	

Veiled Chameleon
(Chamaeleo calyptratus)

Chapter Three

LIZARDS

There are more than 6,700 species of lizards, a diverse and widespread group of reptiles. Many lizard species live in tropical regions around the world, but others have adapted to different habitats and ecosystems across the globe. Some species live in the hottest deserts, while others make their homes as far north as the Arctic Circle.

Anatomy

What do lizards have in common with other reptiles? They are covered in scales, are ectothermic, and lay eggs. Yet, you can easily tell a lizard apart from other reptile species based on some general characteristics. Most lizards have four legs and a long tail. Some lizards, like skinks, have very small legs and use their body to slither on their bellies like a snake. There are even lizards that have no legs at all. Usually, lizards have eyelids and external openings for ears, but not always. For example, most geckos do not have eyelids—they keep their eyes clean by licking them!

What They Eat

Most lizard species tend to eat other animals, from insects to mammals as large as a deer. But there are also species that eat only plants, like the green iguana, and some that are omnivores—they eat everything. One example is the bearded dragon; while this lizard usually eats plants, it will never turn down a juicy bug that passes by.

Skin and Scales

Lizards come in a variety of colors—from green to dark brown to brilliant orange—and range in size from tiny chameleons that fit on your pinky to the Komodo dragon, the world's largest lizard (it's longer than a compact car). Some lizards even have spots like a leopard. These colors help them communicate with other lizards. Other lizards, such as chameleons, are masters of camouflage; their color pattern helps them to blend into their surroundings. There are even venomous lizards, like the Gila monster!

Chameleons blending into their surroundings

Reptiles in the Wild

Many conservation issues threaten lizards around the world; these issues include habitat loss, climate change, and human impact. Fortunately, there are many wildlife conservation projects dedicated to protecting lizards, too.

On the tropical Caribbean island of Grand Cayman lives a large, bright blue iguana. The impressive blue iguana (*Cyclura lewisi*) can grow up to five feet long, weighs 25 pounds, and lives as long as a human! Speeding cars and feral cats and dogs almost drove this lizard to extinction, but thanks to the Blue Iguana Conservation Program, there is hope for this big, blue iguana. Their captive breeding program has helped reintroduce this lizard into the wild and to increase its population.

Blue Iguana
(Cyclura lewisi)

REPTILES AT HOME

Lizards are among the most common reptiles we can see outdoors. Many species, like the western fence lizard (*Sceloporus occidentalis*) and the green iguana (*Iguana iguana*), are active during the day when we can watch their interesting behaviors.

If you want to study lizards more closely at home, the calm leopard gecko and the inquisitive bearded dragon are both bred in captivity and can thrive in these conditions. Your local animal shelter may even have a **leopard gecko** or **bearded dragon** that you can adopt! These reptiles require different care; you'll have to do plenty of research to maintain these incredible beasts.

It might be hard to keep a lizard at home, but you could build an outdoor habitat that wild lizards will love. Encouraging lizards to live in your backyard is easy and fun. Lizards like places to hide, but they also like a nice place to sit and bask in the sun. Building a "lizard wall" (a small wall of stacked rocks and stone) will encourage lizards to visit your backyard or provide a home for the lizards that already live there. Lizards make great neighbors and will keep pesky insects away from a garden.

Bearded Dragon

Pogona vitticeps

SAY IT! *poh-GO-na vit-TEH-sepps*

The bearded dragon is a medium-size lizard from Australia. Most bearded dragons will grow about as long as an adult's forearm. You might wonder, does this reptile really have a beard? It does! The underside of its throat turns from light-tan to dark-brown whenever the lizard is threatened or stressed. It will also puff up its whole body and extend its "beard" to make it look bigger than it really is.

These sun-loving reptiles are active during the day and can often be seen basking out on trees, rocks, and even fence posts. Bearded dragons are tough lizards, but they have a gentle disposition, which makes them popular to exhibit in zoos and to keep as pets.

REPTILE STATS

FAMILY NAME: Agamidae (uh-GAM-uh-dee)

HABITAT: Deserts, shrublands, and woodlands in Australia

SIZE: Up to 2 feet

COLOR: Ranges from sandy brown to yellow and red-orange

DIET: Insects, mammals, and vegetation

Blue-Tongued Skink

Tiliqua gigas

SAY IT! *till-EE-kwah GIG-us*

The blue-tongued skink is named for its big, blue tongue. Scientists are not entirely sure why exactly their tongues are blue, but it might be a way to frighten away predators. When this lizard is threatened, it will open its mouth and stick out its blue tongue!

The skinks have small legs and big, long bodies. They use their little legs to move forward, and drag their belly scales on the ground as they do. They are omnivores and feed on a variety of different foods. Blue-tongued skinks are usually very calm and these gentle reptiles are great to study under captive conditions.

REPTILE STATS

FAMILY NAME: Scincidae (SKIN-kuh-DEE)

HABITAT: Woodlands, semi-desert and scrublands in Australia, Papua New Guinea and Indonesia

SIZE: Up to 2 feet

COLOR: Gray-brown, cream, or orange-red bodies with bands across the back and tail

DIET: Vegetation, insects, and small mammals

Jackson's Chameleon

Trioceros jacksonii

SAY IT! *TRY-ah-ser-OSE JAK-suh-NEE-eye*

These excellent climbers and hunters are adapted for a life in the trees. Chameleons have feet similar to a parrot's: Their toes stick out to the side in pairs, which allows them to grip branches with ease. Visual hunters, they use their incredible eyes to spot insects from 15 to 30 feet away. When they get close to their prey, they shoot out their long tongue to grab them. A chameleon's tongue can be as long as its body, so some have a tongue almost as long as an adult forearm!

Many chameleon species have bumpy, large structures (or even horns) on their head or nose. The Jackson's chameleon has three horns, which the males use to fight with each other over females.

REPTILE STATS

FAMILY NAME: Chamaeleonidae (kuh-MEE-lee-ON-uh-dee)

HABITAT: Forests, woodlands, and deserts in Africa and South Asia

SIZE: Up to 2 feet

COLOR: Varies from green to dark brown to turquoise blue, with the ability to change color

DIET: Insects and small vertebrates

Crested Gecko

Correlophus ciliatus

SAY IT! *KOR-al-OH-fuhs SILL-ee-AH-tuhs*

This fascinating gecko from the island New Caledonia is found nowhere else in the world. These **arboreal** geckos get their name from the rows of tiny pointed scales above their eyes (they are also called eye-lash geckos). When frightened, this lizard can drop its tail! The tail drops and flops around, distracting predators as the gecko escapes to safety. Unlike most lizards, crested geckos' tails do not grow back. But while the gecko might lose some of its balance, it is perfectly okay without its tail.

The crested gecko is now a popular pet and can live for a long time. Some have lived for 20 years.

REPTILE STATS

FAMILY NAME: Diplodactylidae (DIP-low-DAK-till-LEH-dee)

HABITAT: The islands around New Caledonia

SIZE: Up to 11 inches

COLOR: Yellow, tan, red-brown to dark brown with patterns on the back

DIET: Insects, nectar, and fruit

Leopard Gecko

Eublepharis macularius

SAY IT! *YOU-bleh-FAIR-us MAH-cue-LAR-ee-us*

The ground-dwelling leopard gecko is native to northwest India, Nepal, Pakistan, Afghanistan, and Iran. In the cold of winter, the gecko will seek shelter and burrow in the ground to brumate. Fortunately, they can survive off of the fat stored in their thick tails. Their tails have many uses. When threatened, the leopard gecko can drop its tail, which distracts the predator and lets the gecko escape. The tail will grow back, although it will be stunted and will not look the same as the original tail.

The leopard gecko gets its name from its beautiful spotted pattern, which is similar to a leopard's coat. This lizard has a calm nature, which makes it a popular pet.

REPTILE STATS

FAMILY NAME: Eublepharidae (YOU-bleh-FAIR-ee-dee)

HABITAT: Rock grasslands and deserts

SIZE: Up to 11 inches

COLOR: Bodies range from yellow to brown with dark spots

DIET: Insects

Argus Monitor Lizard

Varanus panoptes

SAY IT! *vuh-RAN-uhs pan-OP-tees*

The monitor lizard is one of 80 species in the genus *Varanus*. Their powerful tails, strong limbs, and long necks help them run fast, swim far, and climb high. Most monitor lizards are big—some species are more than eight feet long—and are brown to gray, though some have beautifully colored bands or spots. These active hunters will chase down anything that can fit in their mouth. Some species even eat fruit!

These highly observant lizards are very curious; they constantly "monitor," or watch, anything that might be of interest or a threat. To get a better view of its surroundings, the Argus monitor will "tripod"—raise itself up on its hind legs and use its tail to support its body!

REPTILE STATS

FAMILY NAME: Varanidae (vuh-RAN-uh-dee)

HABITAT: Forests, woodlands, deserts throughout Africa, Asia, and Australia

SIZE: Up to 8 feet

COLOR: Ranges from brown to red or yellow with intricate patterns

DIET: Insects, crustaceans, mammals, birds, amphibians, reptiles, fish, and fruit

Gila Monster

Heloderma suspectum

SAY IT! *HEE-loh-DER-muh suh-SPEK-tum*

The desert-dwelling Gila monster is a large, slow-moving lizard that has thick, studded skin that helps to protect it from predators, like coyotes and raptors. These carnivorous lizards eat all types of prey, but finding food in the desert can be difficult. Fortunately, this lizard has a slow metabolism—it only needs to eat five to 10 times per year.

The Gila monster is named after the Gila River Basin in Arizona and New Mexico. But why is it called a "monster"? Early settlers in the southwest thought the Gila monster had toxic breath! Though this lizard is venomous, it only produces a small amount of venom at a time and its bite is usually not fatal to humans.

REPTILE STATS

FAMILY NAME: Helodermatidae (HEE-loh-der-MAT-uh-dee)

HABITAT: Deserts of southwest United States and northwest Mexico

SIZE: Up to 2 feet

COLOR: Orange or pink body with black reticulating, or netlike, pattern

DIET: Mammals, amphibians, reptiles, birds, and eggs

Green Iguana

Iguana iguana

SAY IT! *ih-GWON-uh ih-GWON-uh*

Iguanas are large, herbivorous lizards from the Americas. These sun-loving reptiles are active during the day and some species, such as the green iguana (*Iguana iguana*), can be seen basking out in the open: in trees, on rocks, and even in public parks.

These lizards are known for their third eye (called a **parietal eye**), which rests on the top of their head. The parietal eye is an organ that looks like a clear, oval scale; it can detect changes in light, which tell the iguana whether it's day or night.

While some iguana species are omnivores, most eat plants. Their small, serrated teeth help to hold onto and tear into their favorite plant snack.

REPTILE STATS

FAMILY NAME: Iguanidae (ih-GWON-uh-dee)

HABITAT: Forests throughout Mexico, and Central and South America

SIZE: Up to 6 feet

COLOR: Bright green, green-brown, dark brown to dark gray

DIET: Flowers, cacti, plants; some species are omnivores

Komodo Dragon

Varanus komodoensis

SAY IT! *vuh-RAN-uhs koh-MOH-doh-en-suhs*

Komodo dragons are the world's largest lizard species. While all Komodo dragons are big, the males are larger than females. The average adult male Komodo dragon is eight feet long and weighs 175 to 200 pounds—that's 25 to 50 pounds heavier than a female.

These lizards are named after their home island of Komodo in Indonesia, and are so strong that they can swim between the neighboring islands with ease. However, since they live only on these islands, the Komodo dragon is considered a threatened species. Fortunately, the Indonesian government protects this amazing reptile; Komodo National Park was founded to conserve their population.

REPTILE STATS

FAMILY NAME: Varanidae (vuh-RAN-uh-dee)

HABITAT: Forests and woodlands on the island of Komodo, Indonesia

SIZE: Up to 8 feet long

COLOR: Dark brown

DIET: Mammals, birds, and reptiles

Hermann's Tortoise
(Testudo hermanni)

Chapter Four

TURTLES AND TORTOISES

Thanks to the fossil record, we know that the first turtle-like reptile species, *Eunotosaurus africanus*, lived on earth about 250 million years ago. These reptiles survived mass extinctions—and even dinosaurs. Today there are more than 350 species of turtles and tortoises.

Even though they look very different, turtles and tortoises have a lot in common with other reptiles: They have four limbs, they are ectothermic, their bodies have scales, and they all lay eggs. What makes turtles and tortoises unique among all reptiles is their shell.

Shells

The shell is made of bony plates that are the animal's ribs and vertebrae. The shell itself is covered either in hard scales, called **scutes**, or a leathery skin. There are two parts to the shell: the top of the shell is called the **carapace** and the bottom of the shell (the belly) is called the **plastron**. The carapace and the plastron work together and act like a suit of armor that protects the turtle or tortoise from predators. On the front of the plastron are two scales called the gular scutes (or the gular horns). In male tortoises, these scutes are very large and they are used to flip other males on their backs when they are fighting over a female!

Bony plates

The top of the shell is called the carapace

The bottom is called the plastron

Big and Small

Some species are small, such as the common musk turtle (*Sternotherus odoratus*), which has a carapace about four inches long. But other species are huge; for example, Galápagos tortoises (genus *Chelonoidis*) can weigh a whopping 500 pounds and have a shell that is four feet long! These sizes vary as a result of the different habitats and ecosystems where turtles and tortoises live.

Galápagos Giant Tortoise *(Chelonoidis nigra)*

Where They Live

Most turtle species are great swimmers and spend their lives in rivers, ponds, and even oceans. Others, like the eastern box turtle, live on land. Tortoises live on land and even thrive in harsh environments like the desert. The environment in which turtles and tortoises live also shapes their behavior. Water-loving turtles will swim away from a predator, while a tortoise will hunker down inside its shell for protection.

Turtles and tortoises live a long time. In fact, tortoises are the longest living animal on land—some have even lived more than 150 years!

Reptiles in the Wild

Of all the reptile species, turtles and tortoises are some of the most endangered due to habitat loss, pollution, and human interference. Luckily, there are many ways you can help.

Many conservation organizations are committed to helping these reptiles. If you live along the eastern coast of the United States, there may be a local organization that protects sea turtles, like the leatherback sea turtle. You can sign up for a beach cleanup and help remove plastic and other debris. Some sea turtles mistake the floating plastic for food, and keeping our waterways clean helps protect these animals.

The Sea Turtle Conservancy is the oldest sea turtle conservation organization in the world, and you'll find many important ways you can help sea turtles on their website. You can also support their sea turtle research and conservation programs by virtually adopting a turtle.

Leatherback Sea Turtle
(Dermochelys coriacea)

REPTILES AT HOME

Turtles and tortoises are amazing reptiles, and some may even be cruising through your neighborhood. Where can you find one? In the southeastern United States, look for the **eastern box turtle** (*Terrapene carolina carolina*) and the gopher tortoise (*Gopherus polyphemus*). In the southwest deserts, you might find a desert tortoise (*Gopherus agassizii*). In waterways across the United States, keep your eyes open for pond turtles and sliders basking on logs and rocks.

Turtles and tortoises can live inside people's homes, but they require committed and expert care for decades. Search online to find your local herpetological society or animal shelter, which often has turtles and tortoises available to adopt. Some tortoises, like the large African sulcata tortoise, will grow too big to live indoors. However, species like the Russian tortoise and the eastern box turtle stay small as they age.

Reptiles like their space. If you keep one at home, build a turtle or tortoise garden in your backyard to give them room to roam around. But if you don't have a lot of space, visit your local zoo, which is sure to have incredible exhibits that highlight these amazing reptiles.

African Sulcata Tortoise

Centrochelys sulcata

SAY IT! *CEN-tro-CHEL-ees sul-CAA-taa*

The African sulcata tortoise is the third-largest tortoise in the world; adults can weigh more than 200 pounds. This tortoise thrives in the arid regions of Africa, where it survives by eating grasses and plants found in this dry habitat. To escape the desert heat, the tortoise digs a deep burrow, which eventually becomes a home for other animals. The tortoise is also called the African spurred tortoise, named for the large "spurs" on the side of its feet. These spurs are hardened scales that help protect them from predators. When threatened, the tortoise retreats into its shell and sticks out these spurs like spikes.

Their large size makes these tortoises hard to keep as pets. Visit a local zoo to study these large reptiles up close.

REPTILE STATS

FAMILY NAME: Testudinidae (TES-tyoo-DIN-uh-dee)

HABITAT: Deserts and savannahs in northern Africa

SIZE: Carapace size is up to 33 inches

COLOR: Yellow to tan carapace

DIET: Grasses, succulents, and other vegetation

Russian Tortoise

Agrionemys horsfieldii

SAY IT! *AG-ree-OH-nem-ees HORSE-fee-ELD-aye*

The small Russian tortoise is native to countries throughout Central Asia. These tortoises have a carapace about five to ten inches long (the females are a little larger than the males) and they can live for a long time—some are 100 years old! Because it lives in cold climates, this reptile spends a lot of time sleeping! Russian tortoises are known to brumate for nine months out of the year to escape the frigid winter temperatures.

This species has also been to space! In 1968, Russian scientists sent two Russian tortoises to the moon aboard the Russia Zond 5 space mission. The spacecraft orbited the moon and returned the tortoises safely back to Earth.

REPTILE STATS

FAMILY NAME: Testudinidae (TES-tyoo-DIN-uh-dee)

HABITAT: Deserts and grasslands in central Asia

SIZE: Carapace size is up to 10 inches

COLOR: Tan to brown carapace

DIET: Vegetation and succulents

Leopard Tortoise

Stigmochelys pardalis

SAY IT! *STIG-moh-CHEL-ees par-DAL-us*

Leopard tortoises live in a variety of dry habitats and can be found at high elevations and at sea level. These tortoises are active all year but will sometimes seek shelter (such as burrows made by other animals) to escape colder temperatures. They eat grasses, succulents, and other vegetation within reach of the ground. An adult leopard tortoise can weigh up to 80 pounds, which makes it the fourth-largest tortoise in the world.

The leopard tortoise is a beautiful reptile. When young, this tortoise's carapace is patterned with black spots and blotches on a yellow background, which looks like a leopard's coat. The pattern fades with age.

REPTILE STATS

FAMILY NAME: Testudinidae (TES-tyoo-DIN-uh-dee)

HABITAT: Savannahs and grasslands across eastern and southern Africa

SIZE: Carapace size is up to 28 inches

COLOR: Yellow carapace with black blotches and spots

DIET: Grasses, succulents, and other vegetation

Red-eared Slider

Trachemys scripta elegans

SAY IT! *TRACK-em-ees SCRIPT-ah EL-ee-gans*

The red-eared slider is native to the southeastern United States, but it lives all over the world. It gets its name from the colorful red stripes on the sides of its head. Thanks to its broad, webbed feet, this excellent swimmer thrives in water. It can hunt fish and other animals, but it also eats plants.

This turtle species can grow quite large and it needs to live in water, so they are difficult to keep as pets. When they grow too big for an owner to keep, they are often released in places where they may become invasive and cause harm to other wildlife.

REPTILE STATS

FAMILY NAME: Emydidae (EM-i-di-dee)

HABITAT: Freshwater ponds, rivers, and lakes in the southeastern United States

SIZE: Carapace size is up to 16 inches

COLOR: Brown and green carapace, bright yellow to tan plastron

DIET: Fish, amphibians, and vegetation

Eastern Box Turtle

Terrapene carolina carolina

SAY IT! *ter-ROP-uh-nee KAR-uh-LINE-uh KAR-uh-LINE-uh*

The unique eastern box turtle has a hinged plastron that can open and close, like a box! When threatened, this turtle tucks its head, legs, and tail inside its body; then it pulls the hinged plastron shut. The turtle hides inside the "box" of its hard shell, which protects it from predators. These omnivores use their sharp, horned beaks to eat mushrooms, berries, insects, and even worms. Though the eastern box turtle is not a good swimmer (it may drown if submerged in water), it can live on land where it thrives on the forest floor.

Though it is small, the eastern box turtle requires lots of space to live (and can live for decades). These turtles do much better in the wild than inside a home.

REPTILE STATS

FAMILY NAME: Emydidae (uh-MID-uh-dee)

HABITAT: Forests, woodlands, and grasslands in the United States

SIZE: Carapace size is up to 7 inches

COLOR: Brown or black carapace with red to orange pattern

DIET: Mushrooms, fruits, vegetation, and arthropods

Leatherback Sea Turtle

Dermochelys coriacea

SAY IT! *DER-muh-KEL-eez KOH-ree-ah-SEE-uh*

The leatherback sea turtle is the world's largest turtle. It weighs more than a ton! When you live in the ocean, it pays to be big. Their large size protects them from predators and helps their bodies retain heat. Their unique shell is covered in thick, leathery skin that is rubbery and tough.

The leatherback sea turtle lives in oceans around the world—even in the Arctic Ocean. These outstanding swimmers have large flippers on their front and hind limbs. They don't rest much; instead, they constantly produce energy to warm their body—by swimming! Leatherback sea turtles will spend most of their lives in the ocean, but females return to sandy beaches to lay their eggs.

REPTILE STATS

FAMILY NAME: Dermochelyidae (DER-muh-kuh-LY-uh-dee)

HABITAT: Oceans

SIZE: Carapace size is up to 7 feet

COLOR: Gray to dark gray carapace

DIET: Jellyfish and soft-bodied organisms

Nile Crocodile
(Crocodylus niloticus)

Chapter Five

CROCODILES AND ALLIGATORS

Crocodiles and alligators are an ancient group of reptiles called crocodilians. They belong to an order called Crocodilia that also includes the alligator-like caimans, from the Americas, and the fish-eating gharials of South Asia. How ancient are these reptiles? The first crocodile-like fossil is almost 250 million years old. That means that crocodilians (and their ancestors) have been around since before the time of the dinosaurs!

These reptiles are mostly tropical, though some species thrive in cooler regions like in the southeastern United States and China. All crocodilians have adapted to living in water and are excellent swimmers.

Anatomy

Crocodilians resemble lizards—they all have four legs and a tail—but they are very different. They walk with their body (and most of their tail) high above the ground, unlike other reptiles, which crawl. This is because their legs sit almost directly underneath their body. Their ankle joints are also different from those of other reptiles. Though they usually walk slowly, crocodilians can make sudden bursts of speed and can even gallop.

These reptiles lay eggs, and many species will defend their nests against predators. Some will even stay with their young after they hatch. When the baby crocodilians grow up, they will find their own place to live. Most crocodilians are fiercely territorial—they will fight each other for the best place to live—so most crocodilians prefer to live alone.

How can you tell the difference between an alligator and a crocodile? Though they are closely related, there are a few differences. First, look at the head. Alligators and caimans have broad snouts, while the snout of a crocodile is much more slender. When their jaws are closed, a crocodile looks like it has a toothy grin; all its teeth are visible. Alligators have a larger upper jaw than their bottom jaw, so their teeth stay mostly hidden.

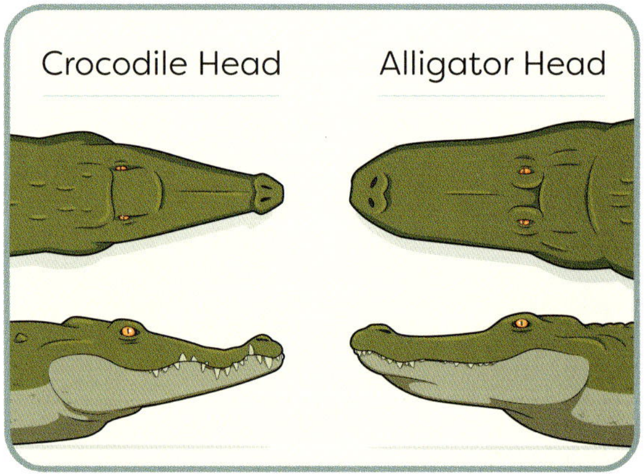

Skin and Scales

Crocodilians are covered in a skin of thick scales that do not overlap. Their water-tight skin allows them to move in and out of the water with ease. On their back and neck are hard bony plates, called osteo-derms. Osteoderms sit under the scales and act like armor, protecting them from predators and other crocodilians.

Crocodile osteoderms

What They Eat

Crocodilians are predators and some species are at the top of the food chain. When crocodilians spy their prey at the water's edge, they will slowly swim toward it. Once they're within striking distance, they use their large, powerful tails to help propel them as they spring out of the water, ambushing their prey and latching on with their powerful bite. The crocodilian then drags the prey underneath the water to drown.

Saltwater Crocodile
(Crocodylus porosus)

Reptiles in the Wild

Crocodilians are some of the most impressive reptiles in the world. Their large size and predatory nature make us naturally curious about these incredible reptiles. If you are a budding herpetologist and live in the southeastern United States, then chances are you have already seen an alligator. If not, then make seeing one a priority. Luckily there are many protected areas, like the Everglades National Park, where alligators are protected and are easy to see in the wild.

Many crocodilians live in aquatic environments where human development can threaten their habitat. Increased protection of our waterways helps conserve the habitat of many different species. When we visit protected areas like the Everglades National Park, it tells our governments that these habitats are important and that we want them to be saved.

CAIMANS

Caimans are a group of crocodilian species that live in freshwater habitats in Mexico and Central and South America. Caimans are close relatives of alligators and they look very much alike. They have a broad snout, scales, and rows of armored osteoderms, but they are much smaller and usually only reach four to eight feet long. Caimans tend to be much more agile than alligators.

The black caiman (*Melanosuchus niger*) is the largest of all caiman species; they can grow to more than 16 feet long. This predator lives in the Amazon in South America and eats mostly fish, but will also snack on amphibians, insects, birds, and mammals. As an adult, caimans have few, but powerful, predators such as anacondas and jaguars.

American Alligator

Alligator mississippiensis

SAY IT! *AL-uh-GAY-der MIS-uh-SIP-ee-EN-suhs*

The American alligator is native to the United States, where it lives in freshwater lakes, rivers, swamps, and ponds. American alligators reproduce by laying eggs. A female alligator creates a nest of plants and mud, then lays her eggs in the nest and buries them. When the eggs hatch, she carries her babies to the water. When the babies get big, they travel to find their own home.

American alligators grow quite big (males can weigh nearly 1,000 pounds) and are predators. They have been known to attack humans, so it is important to be careful around waterways where they live. But while alligators may be dangerous, they nevertheless almost went extinct! The Endangered Species Act helped save this fierce reptile, and their populations are now thriving.

REPTILE STATS

FAMILY: Alligatoridae (AL-uh-guh-TOR-uh-dee)

HABITAT: Freshwater lakes, rivers, and waterways in the southeastern United States

SIZE: Up to 15 feet

COLOR: Dark olive and brown to black

DIET: Mammals, birds, reptiles, amphibians, and arthropods

Nile Crocodile

Crocodylus niloticus

SAY IT! *KRAH-kuh-DIL-uhs NY-lah-TIH-kuhs*

The large Nile crocodile lives in freshwater rivers, lakes, and ponds throughout Africa. This ambush predator sneaks up on its prey and captures it. When the crocodile is young and small, the prey it eats are also small: mostly insects, amphibians, birds, and small mammals. As the crocodile grows larger, it eats prey as big as a zebra or gazelle!

Nile crocodiles are often seen together and can live in large groups. However, size matters. The largest male crocodiles are the top crocs; they take the best basking spots and get to eat first. If that hierarchy is not respected, the crocodiles will fight, which can be violent and even fatal.

REPTILE STATS

FAMILY: Crocodylidae (KRAH-kuh-DIL-uh-dee)

HABITAT: Rivers, lakes, and ponds throughout Africa

SIZE: Up to 16 feet

COLOR: Dark tan, brown, and gray

DIET: Mammals, birds, reptiles, amphibians, fish

Saltwater Crocodile

Crocodylus porosus

SAY IT! *KRAH-kuh-DIL-uhs POR-oh-suhs*

The saltwater crocodile is the largest crocodile species and is one of the largest reptiles in the world. While an adult female can be 13 feet long and weigh 300 to 400 pounds, the much larger adult male can reach 20 feet long and weigh more than 2,000 pounds! These big predators also have a big bite thanks to the huge muscles that are attached to their skull and bulge at the base of their head. This allows them to take down prey like deer and wild pigs and easily snap bones.

This crocodile spends lots of time in salty and brackish water, but it can live in fresh water, too. They can stay in the same place for a long time but can also swim long distances and even into the open ocean. Their powerful tails help propel them easily through the water.

REPTILE STATS

FAMILY: Crocodylidae (KRAH-kuh-DIL-uh-dee)

HABITAT: Mangroves, brackish lagoons, coastal waterbodies across Southeast Asia and Australia

SIZE: Up to 20 feet

COLOR: Grayish green to tan

DIET: Mammals, birds, reptiles, amphibians, fish, crustaceans

ARE DINOSAURS REPTILES?

Hundreds of millions of years ago, early reptiles dominated the planet. Through millions of years of evolution, some of those ancient reptiles began to change into dinosaurs. **Paleontologists**, scientists who study dinosaurs, think that dinosaurs branched off from a subgroup of reptiles called archosaurs more than 200 million years ago. Dinosaurs belong to the **clade** Dinosauria, which is a part of the class Reptilia. This tells us that dinosaurs are one specific type of reptile.

Other ancient reptiles lived at the same time as dinosaurs. For example, 100 million years ago, a 40-foot-long freshwater crocodile in the genus *Deinosuchus* lived with dinosaurs, and probably ate them!

Red-Eyed Tree Frog
(Agalychnis callidryas)

Chapter Six

AMPHIBIANS

Amphibians are a prehistoric group of animals that have lived on land and in water for millions of years. Here's a cool fact: Though they look very much alike, amphibians are not reptiles. The ancestors of modern amphibians are actually older than the first reptiles by about 30 million years! Today, amphibians are found all over the world (except in Antarctica).

Today there are more than 8,100 species of amphibians that are divided into three orders: frogs and toads, newts and salamanders, and caecilians.

Skin Like a Sponge

The word amphibian means "two lives," and refers to the fact that amphibians live both on land and in water. Their skin is smooth and permeable, which means that the skin acts like a sponge and soaks up moisture from the environment. In a sense, they drink through their skin. Amphibians are ectotherms and predators, but because they are slow moving and do not require much energy, they don't need to hunt for food very often.

Metamorphosis

Amphibians lay soft, jelly-like eggs in water or in a moist place. After the eggs hatch, the babies enter a larval stage (like a tadpole before it becomes a frog). They grow gills and breathe underwater. Then their bodies change; they grow legs, develop lungs, and eventually leave the water to live on land. This process is called metamorphosis and amphibians (and some fish) are the only vertebrates that experience this. They need to keep their skin moist, so they must return to the water or find somewhere wet to rehydrate. If they don't rehydrate, they could dry out or even die.

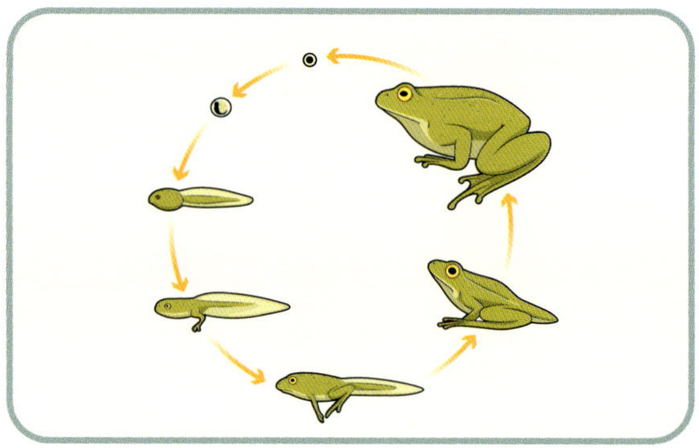

Amphibians in the Wild

Amphibians are incredibly important to humans. They eat pests like flies and mosquitoes. Also, amphibians are bio-indicators: Their highly specialized skin absorbs water and nutrients, but it can also soak up bad things like pollution or pesticides, which can make amphibians sick. As amphibians live on both land and in water, they can show scientists the health of both environments and when they need help.

Amphibians need help from us, too. Habitat loss, disease, pollution, and climate change make it hard for these creatures to survive, and there are fewer and fewer of them. The good news is that there are many ways to help!

- Search online to find a local conservation organization and ask what you can to do to help. You could participate in a cleanup day at some local wetlands or help your household to use fewer pesticides.
- Join your local FrogWatch chapter and become a citizen scientist.
- If you have a backyard, ask an adult or friend to help build a frog pond and give these amazing creatures a cool place to live.

Frogs and Toads

Most of the world's amphibians are frogs and toads. They live everywhere from tropical rain forests to scorching hot deserts. What's the difference between a toad and a frog? A toad is actually a type of frog, but there are a few differences. Toads tend to live in dry places while frogs spend more time in water. Toads have bumpy skin; sometimes people call these "warts," but toads cannot give you warts! On each side of the toad's head, and behind each eye, is a large bump; these are poison glands. If a predator bites the toad on the head, the predator will get a mouthful of toxic poison. Though it's not (usually) fatal to humans, this poison can be very toxic to small predators.

Frogs and toads have two things in common: a short body and no tail. Some species have long legs, which make them great jumpers. The American bullfrog (*Lithobates catesbeianus*) can jump up to six feet!

Red-Eyed Tree Frog

Agalychnis callidryas

SAY IT! *AH-gal-LICK-nuhs CAL-lee-DRY-as*

The beautiful red-eyed tree frog has big, sticky toe pads on their feet that help them climb. They spend most of their lives high up in the canopy of the rain forests.

AMPHIBIAN STATS

FAMILY: Phyllomedusidae (FY-low-MEH-doo-SA-ee-dee)

HABITAT: Rain forests of Central and South America

SIZE: Up to 3 inches

COLOR: Bright green-blue with yellow sides and red eyes

DIET: Insects

Rough-Skinned Newt

Taricha granulosa

SAY IT! *Ta-REE-caa GRAN-you-LOW-sah*

Newts are a type of a salamander that live in North America, Europe, northern Africa, and Asia. They have four limbs and a long tail, which helps them swim. These semi-aquatic amphibians spend part of their lives in water and the other part on land, usually in moist places under fallen logs or deep in burrows and leaf litter. Every year, newts travel to a nearby body of water in order to mate and lay eggs.

When the eggs hatch, these baby newts (or larvae) enter an aquatic stage. The larvae have gills on the side of their head that look almost like feathers. Some newts become efts that live on land; they are brightly colored before turning into aquatic adults.

Most newt species have skin that contains toxins that help to protect them from predators. Most toxins make the newt taste bad and are even poisonous. Newts of the genus Taricha are very toxic—this is the most poisonous salamander in the world! This type of newt displays its brightly colored belly to warm predators of its toxic skin.

AMPHIBIAN STATS

FAMILY: Salamandridae (SAL-ah-MAN-dree-dee)

HABITAT: Coastal forests of the Pacific Northwest

SIZE: Up to 7 inches

COLOR: Dark brown to black backs, bright orange belly

DIET: Insects, worms, invertebrates

Chinese Giant Salamander

Andrias davidianus

SAY IT! *an-DREE-as DA-vid-EE-an-us*

Salamanders look like lizards, but are very different—they are amphibians with tails! They can even re-grow their limbs and tail. Most salamanders live in places with mild temperatures, though some live in the tropics. Different species can be fully aquatic or live on land. Salamanders lay their eggs in water or in moist places, such as under a log or in moss. Many species have aquatic larvae.

Salamanders are predators, but since they move slowly, they must wait for their prey to pass by. When the prey is close, the salamander will strike quickly and bite it. Some salamanders can shoot out their tongue, which sticks to the prey and brings it right into the salamander's mouth.

The Chinese giant salamander is the world's largest salamander, at almost six feet long. This giant can live for more than 60 years and has a strong bite that snaps fish up with ease.

AMPHIBIAN STATS

FAMILY: Cryptobranchidae (KRIP-toe-BRANK-ee-dee)

HABITAT: Freshwater streams in China

SIZE: Up to 6 feet

COLOR: Dark brown to reddish brown

DIET: Crustaceans, insects, fish, small mammals

MORE TO DISCOVER

AmphibiaWeb
AmphibiaWeb.org

Blue Iguana Conservation Program
NationalTrust.org.ky/our-work/conservation/blue-iguana-conservation

Crocodilians
Crocodilian.com

FrogWatch USA
AZA.org/frogwatch

HerpMapper
HerpMapper.org

National Wildlife Federation
NWF.org

The Reptile Database
Reptile-Database.reptarium.cz

Save the Snakes
SaveTheSnakes.org

Sea Turtle Conservancy
ConserveTurtles.org

Turtle Survival Alliance
TurtleSurvival.org

GLOSSARY

AMPHISBAENIANS: Reptiles in the family Amphisbaenidae, which have snake-like bodies and no limbs; also called "worm lizards."

ARBOREAL: Animals that live in trees and are adapted to climbing.

BRUMATION: (brew-MAY-shun) The hibernation-like state exhibited by reptiles during cold weather; garter snakes that live in Canada go into brumation during the winter.

CAPTIVITY: The state of animals held in captive conditions, such as at a zoo or nature center, or as a pet; the Komodo dragons at the zoo were born in captivity.

CARAPACE: The dorsal, or top, part of a turtle or tortoise shell.

CLADE: A taxonomic group of organisms that share features from a common ancestor.

CLASS: A taxonomic rank based on biology; for example, the class of snakes is Reptilia.

DIURNAL: Animals that are active during the day; the bearded dragon is a diurnal reptile.

DORSAL: The scales on the top of the snake.

ECOSYSTEM: (EE-coh-SISS-tem) The habitat where animals, plants, and other organisms live.

ECTOTHERMIC: (EK-toe-THURM-ick) An animal that regulates its body temperature using outside sources; a snake might bask on a rock to warm up under the sun's rays.

EVOLUTION: The process of incremental change of a species' characteristics over many generations.

GENUS: (JEAN-us) A taxonomic rank that defines a group of organisms with similar characteristics.

INCUBATE: The heating of eggs so that they can develop and hatch; alligators build a nest that incubates their eggs.

INTERSTITIAL: Situated within a particular organ or tissue, such as the skin between a snake's scales.

INVASIVE SPECIES: An organism that is not native to an ecosystem and causes negative impacts to that ecosystem; the Burmese python is an example of a snake species that is an invasive species in southern Florida, where it is causing harm to native wildlife.

JACOBSON'S ORGAN: An organ that detects scent molecules in the environment; a snake's Jacobson's organ helps it find prey.

KERATIN: (CARE-a-tin) A protein that is the structure for different parts of the bodies of animals; examples of keratin include scales, horns, hair, and fingernails.

LARVAL: The juvenile stage of an organism before it completes metamorphosis; tadpoles are in their larval stage before they metamorphose into frogs.

LOCOMOTION: The process of physical movement from one place to another.

NATIVE: A species that evolved in the place where it is found; the inland taipan is native to Australia.

NOCTURNAL: Animals that are active at night; many species of geckos are nocturnal and at night will hang out around street lamps to eat insects attracted to the light.

ORDER: A taxonomic rank of organisms; the order of snakes is Squamata.

PARIETAL EYE: A light-sensitive organ that is on top of a lizard's head, in between its eyes.

PLASTRON: The ventral, or bottom, part of a turtle or tortoise shell.

SCUTES: A hard, bony plate on a reptile; tortoise shells are covered in dermal scutes, which protect their bodies from harm.

SUBSPECIES: A subdivision of a species, especially a geographical or ecological subdivision.

TAXONOMY: (TAX-on-OH-me) The branch of science that focuses on classification.

VENTRAL: The scales on the belly of a snake.

VERTEBRATE: Organism with a backbone; humans and reptiles both have backbones and, therefore, are vertebrates.

INDEX

ABOUT THE AUTHOR

Michael G. Starkey is a conservation biologist, ecological consultant, and public speaker working to educate and involve the public in wildlife conservation issues. From collaborating with communities to protect rare frogs in Ghana to tracking Yucatán black howler monkeys in Belize, Michael has worked with a wide diversity of wildlife from around the world. However, his passion has always been focused on snakes and he has worked on projects in California with San Francisco garter snakes, giant garter snakes, and northern Pacific rattlesnakes.

Michael is the founder and executive director of Save The Snakes, a nonprofit organization dedicated to snake conservation. He uses his knowledge, positive attitude, and enthusiasm for snake conservation to engage the public in protecting these beautiful animals. Michael gives educational presentations around the world to inform the public about the threats facing wildlife and to help nurture a society that respects and appreciates nature.